Beginners' Guide to Mastering Coding Essentials.

Felix K. Nguyen

Engage in regular eye check-ups; vision health is crucial and often overlooked.

Stay vigilant about tech's impact on mental health; while it connects us, it also poses challenges like screen addiction.

Engage with literature that promotes resilience; life's challenges are easier faced with inner strength and wisdom.

Life's tapestry is rich with colors; weave it with diverse experiences and perspectives.

Introduction

This book is a comprehensive guide designed to help beginners understand the fundamentals of coding using the Small Basic programming language. Here's an overview of the content covered in the guide:

The guide begins with introductory sections on computers, programs, programming languages, machine language, and the Internet and World Wide Web. These sections lay the foundation for understanding the world of programming.

It then delves into the concept of algorithms, explaining what they are and why they are essential in programming. The guide introduces readers to the five elements of a program, providing insights into the key components needed for writing code effectively.

The primary focus of the guide is on Small Basic, a beginner-friendly programming language. It covers the basics of Small Basic, including coding tips and practical advice for beginners.

Readers are encouraged to start their coding journey with their first assignment in Small Basic. The guide walks them through the process, providing step-by-step instructions and examples.

As readers progress, the guide explores more advanced topics, including variables, mathematical operations, conditional statements, loops, and the use of graphics in Small Basic programs. These sections help readers build a strong foundation in coding.

The guide introduces the concept of subroutines and how they can be used to modularize code. It also covers topics like working with turtles, arrays, and creating basic programs.

Towards the end, the guide explores the concept of events and how they can be incorporated into Small Basic programs.

In summary, this book is a beginner-friendly guide that covers essential programming concepts and techniques using the Small Basic language. It provides readers with a step-by-step approach to learning coding basics, making it a valuable resource for beginners looking to start their coding journey.

Contents

CHAPTER ONE: CODING

Coding refers to the action of entering instructions into computers to make them perform specified actions. A computer is a special type of machine.

Machines are devices (equipment with a purpose; tools) made by humans to get work done. They are usually made out of durable materials like wood, plastic and metal. Normally they have some parts that move and some parts that don't; sometimes they have no moving parts at all. They receive some kind of energy that they use to do their work.

One of the traits that makes people different from animals is their ability to create complex machines.

Usually people create machines because there is some work they want to do that the machine could help them with. The help the machine provides could be to get the work done faster, to do the work with less chance of errors, or to do the work nearly continuously, without the need to stop for food or sleep. There are other reasons people make machines, but it usually comes down to getting more work done in a given amount of time with fewer errors.

As time goes on, machines often get improved or changed to make them more effective or to respond to changes in the area of society where they are used.

Cars, planes, telephones and ovens are all machines.

Again, a computer is just another machine – it's a device made by people to get work done.

Let's take a closer look at computers.

CHAPTER TWO: COMPUTERS

Computers were created to do a simple thing: they take in data (information), change the data in some way, and send out data. That's all.

There are certain truths regarding computers:

1. They are only machines. They are not people.

2. They were created by people and can only act if a person tells them to. Even then, they can only perform actions that a person thought of ahead of time and built into them.

Computers do not have a soul. They cannot think. Everything ever done by a computer was predetermined by humans. Even so-called "artificial intelligence" (computer systems that are able to perform actions that require human intelligence, like being able to recognize sounds and images), or computers that can "learn," only have these abilities because we designed them that way.

As machines, some of the characteristics of computers include the following:

- They handle data. Data is information – such as words, symbols (something written that represents an amount, idea or word), pictures, etc.

- They obey instructions (commands entered into them that perform certain tasks).

- They automate (perform actions without human interaction) tasks that would either take too long for a person to do or be too boring. Keep in mind that these automatic actions were designed by a person.

- They process data. "Process" means to handle something through use of an established (and usually routine) set of procedures. When a computer displays the word "processing", it is saying, "Hold on while I perform some pre-established procedures." Processing refers to "taking actions with data". Searching through words to locate typos would be an example of "processing data".

When data is being processed by a computer, you sometimes see a "progress bar" (a symbol that shows how far along something is) like this:

Or you may see this symbol when data is processed:

This circular symbol is called a "throbber" due to the fact that they originally expanded and contracted in size – i.e., the symbol "throbbed".

The purpose of computers is to take in data, process it and send it out.

When computers perform actions, it is referred to as "executing" or "running." For example, you can run a search on the internet by clicking the search button or you could execute an instruction by pressing enter on your keyboard.

It is important to understand that machines are not life forms. Even though they can perform seemingly miraculous operations, the true source of their products is humankind.

Computers aren't very useful without programs – so let's go over what programs are exactly.

CHAPTER THREE: PROGRAMS

As a noun (thing), code is the written instructions you type into a computer to make programs.

Programs are series of written instructions, entered into a computer, which cause the computer to perform a specific task or tasks. For example, Microsoft® Paint is a program that can be used to create basic illustrations on your computer.

Hardware refers to the physical components of the computer – the parts that can be touched. "Hard" means "solid" or "tangible" (able to be seen and felt), and "ware" means "something created".
The computer screen, mouse, printer and keyboard are all hardware.

The opposite of hardware is software. Software is just another word for "computer program" – sets of instructions that tell a computer what to do. Computer games, like Solitaire, are examples of software.

Another word for computer program or software is "application." These terms are all interchangeable. Though "app" (abbreviation of application) is usually used to refer to programs (applications; software) on a mobile device (like a cell phone).

The word software came about in the 1960s to emphasize the difference between it and computer hardware. Software (programs; applications) are the instructions, while hardware implements the instructions.

Installing a program means to put it into a computer so that the program can execute.

For example, you could install a program by transferring the data from the internet to your computer. In the 1990s, most software was installed using a disk that came in a box and looked something like this:

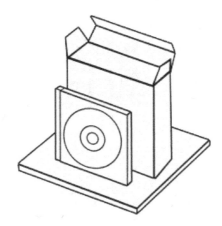

The people that create programs are called computer programmers. They're also referred to as coders, software developers, software engineers and just developers. These position names all mean the same thing.

Programs are created using programming languages, so let's discuss what those are.

CHAPTER FOUR: PROGRAMMING LANGUAGES

Languages are communication systems that allow you to transfer ideas in written and spoken words. Similar to people (like Spanish and English), there are different languages that can be used to write (create) computer programs – these are called programming languages or computer languages. Programming languages are organized systems of words, phrases and symbols that let you create programs.

There are many different types of programming languages, each of which was created to fill a specific purpose. Usually a language is created in order to make the creation of certain types of computer programs easier.

As an example, Python is a popular programming language. This is how you would tell a computer to display the words "Hello, world!" on the screen, using the computer language Python:

print ("Hello, world!")

This is code. All software/applications/programs are made up of code. As a user (the person using something), you don't see the code. The three most common types of programs that developers use to write their code in are:

1) Integrated development environment (IDE): An IDE is a set of programming tools for writing software programs. IDEs are a great aid to computer program creation. An IDE often combines many available tools into one place. Essentially, an IDE is software that helps you make software.

For example, Visual Studio, available from the technology company Microsoft, is one of the many IDEs available for software developers.

IDEs are the most common programs used by developers to write their code.

2) Text editor: A text editor is a program used to write and edit text. Text editors are very basic – meaning, the text is typically plain with no effects. This is technically different from a word processor, which is a program on a computer that allows you to create, format (design the style and layout), modify, and print documents. While text editors can be used to write code, word processors cannot. Instead, word processors have more functionality (ability to perform a wider array of actions) than text editors.

As an example of each, Microsoft Word (on the left) is a word processor, while Notepad (on the right) is a text editor.

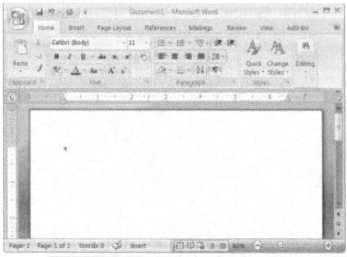

Out of the three programs listed here used to write code within, text editors are the least popular and least recommended.

3) Code editor: As the name states, this is a program that can be used to write/edit your code. Code editors are in between IDEs and text editors in terms of features (functions built into an application) – they have fewer features than an IDE but more than a text editor. One of the most popular code editors is Notepad++ (plus plus).

As an example, the popular IDE Visual Studio has a feature called "LiveShare," which allows developers to share their code with others as it's being written. Other developers can even use LiveShare within Visual Studio to access and edit your code from a separate computer! This feature is not included in the code editor Notepad++.

On the other hand, Notepad++ has a cool feature called "auto-completion" that suggests various options for completing the code you're typing for you. For example, when you type *pr*, auto-completion may suggest *print*. This feature doesn't exist in the text editor Notepad.

As a verb (action), coding means typing out instructions (using a particular programming language) to make a program that will make the computer perform certain actions. It also refers to the creation of websites. Developers usually code in an IDE, code editor or text editor.

Everything in computers comes down to 1s and 0s. Let's see how and why that is.

CHAPTER FIVE: MACHINE LANGUAGE

You may have heard the concept that computers operate on 1s and 0s. How this works exactly is beyond the scope of this book, but a simplified explanation is that computers are made up of billions of tiny parts that can either be on or off. 1 represents on, 0 represents off. You can instruct computers to turn these parts on and off by entering 1 and 0 into the computer. These 1s and 0s are called machine language. Commands written in machine language are called machine instructions.

As an example, "10010100 01101011 01011011 01010110" could instruct the computer to "Delete the file called Vacation.doc." The "10010100 01101011 01011011 01010110" is a machine instruction.

It is difficult for people to read and write in machine language, since the instructions are just unique patterns of ones and zeroes. That is why programming languages were created.
The computer converts (translates) the code written by developers into machine instructions.

It works like this:

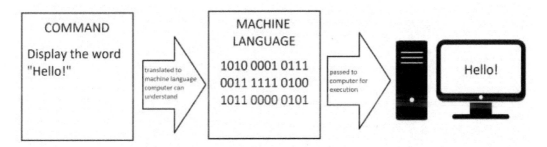

One of the main uses of computers is the internet. So, let's go over what that is exactly.

CHAPTER SIX: THE INTERNET AND WORLD WIDE WEB

The World Wide Web (abbreviated "www" or the "web") is a collection of linked electronic documents, organized into groups called websites.

A website is composed of one or more individual webpages, where a "page" is an organized, separate document containing text, images, video and other elements.

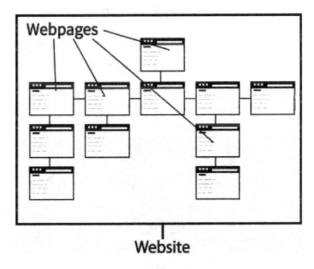

Website

THE INTERNET

A network is a system where two or more computers are connected to each other. The computers can be connected by a cable (i.e., a wired connection) or connected wirelessly (through the air). Network is the word used to describe the link between things that are working together and is used in many different ways with computers. Information can be shared from computer to computer through the use of a network.

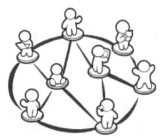

Internet is a combination of the words "interconnected" and "network."

The internet is an interconnected network of many computers around the world. It is the largest network in existence and allows computers to pass data to one another.

There are lots of different types of data that can be sent back and forth between computers connected to the internet – like electronic messages, electronic documents, healthcare records, etc.

In addition to referring to the connection between computers on this network, internet also means the set of agreements, or protocols, for how to transfer different types of data between those computers.

A "protocol" is an official procedure. In technology, it is a formal description of how a certain type of information will be formatted and handled. Basically, it's an agreement that the various people who work with that type of information all adhere to. Protocols are usually described in written documents, and are very precise. They are usually created by experts in the applicable industry.

An example of a type of data where a protocol would be valuable is healthcare information. If various organizations in the healthcare industry were to transfer healthcare data back and forth between computers as they perform their work, it would be important that they all agree about things like the exact format of the information, how to keep private data safe, etc. All of that would be laid down in a written protocol. Several such protocols do exist in the healthcare industry.

One or more protocols have been created for each type of data that can be transferred around on the internet. Violation of these protocols results in an error and the data will not be sent properly or at all.

So to recap: the internet is an interconnected network of many computers around the world, and a set of agreements, or protocols, for transferring different types of data between those computers.

INTERNET VS. WORLD WIDE WEB

So, what's the difference between the internet and the World Wide Web? The internet is the hardware and protocols that data is sent across, whereas the web is one type of information that is accessed over the internet. The web is a collection of linked electronic documents called webpages.

The internet is the infrastructure (physical framework) while the web is the code that is transmitted and displayed. In a way, the internet is the hardware and the web is the software.

Dynamic refers to actions that take place the moment they are needed, rather than in advance. For example, a restaurant that prepares your food to your specifications when you order, would be dynamic. The opposite of dynamic is "static," which literally means, "unchanging." A static restaurant would have food pre-cooked and waiting before you order – the food doesn't change in regards to time or circumstance.

In coding, dynamic means the computer processes your request right when you ask it to – it does not have a predetermined result ahead of time.

Dynamic relates to the internet by describing websites that have content that changes while the website is being viewed.

These are mouse pointers:

As an example, a dynamic picture on a website could be one that has an effect (movement or change) when you hover over it with a mouse (hovering with a mouse refers to holding the pointer over a particular object).

PROGRAMMING

Programming (the action of creating computer programs by writing code; coding) is a spectacular thing because it is one of the few skills that apply to virtually all industries.

Yes, companies that create software definitely utilize coding the most – but if you think about it, most industries utilize technology (software, websites, databases, etc.). And so, coders are valuable assets for companies in any industry – construction, food service, retail, transportation, etc.

There are many, many programming languages, and technology is ever-changing. The whole thing can be quite overwhelming, but there are basics that apply across the vast landscape of technology.

HIGH-LEVEL

Machine language that we discussed earlier (1s and 0s) is considered a "low-level language." This is due to the fact that it is close to the hardware of the computer in that it directly represents the on or off states used in both the computer instructions and the data the computer operates on.

The opposite of a low-level language is a high-level language – code written in a way that is easier to read and write because it somewhat resembles English, such as:

Print "Hello";

Here, you are telling the computer to write out the word Hello on the screen.

All the most popular programming languages are high-level languages – meaning, they use English letters, symbols and words.

DATA TYPES

Data is information.

There are different types of data that computer programs will need. These are data types like:

- Numbers,
- Letters,
- Dates,
- True or false, etc.

When information is used in a computer, that information will have a "data type." This is two things:

1. "What kind of information is this?," and
2. "What kind of things can we do with this data?"

Different data types can be used in different ways.

When data is stored in a computer, its type is also stored – that way the computer knows how to work with that particular piece of data.

The various different things you can do with data are called operations. Not all data types have the same operations available to them.

For example, a "decimal number" (0-9) is a data type. Typical operations you could do with decimal number data are addition, subtraction, multiplication, etc.

"Text" is another data type. Typical operations you could do with text data are "convert the text to uppercase" or "concatenate" (which means to link together, as in a chain – for example, you could take the individual text elements "Pizza" and "s!" and then concatenate them into "Pizzas!" etc.).

When creating computer programs, every piece of data being kept track of by the computer is a certain data type. For example, the datum 342.98 is data of type "decimal." The datum "casserole" is data of type "text."

A B C   1 2 3   TRUE/FALSE   3.14
(examples of data types)

It would not make sense to apply mathematical operations to text data – for example, trying to tell a computer to add the number 34 to the text "banana" wouldn't work because the two types of data are different, and mathematics doesn't apply to text data.

In math, a variable is a symbol used to represent an unknown quantity or a quantity that may change. In computers, a variable is a construct (an idea formed from simpler elements) used to store data that may change as the computer performs its tasks.

Computers often have to keep track of various pieces of information. These can be things like the name of a computer user, the color of the background shown on the computer screen, an order number for something a user ordered from a company, etc.

The computer usually gives each of these pieces of data a NAME and a VALUE. The NAME is used to identify the exact piece of data, and the VALUE is used to show the actual data we need to keep track of. Usually the "=" symbol is used to set the VALUE of a variable.

In math, a value is a numeric amount, quantity, or number – like this: $X = 10$

Here we are saying that the *name* "X" holds the *value* of "10."

In coding, a value is any sort of characteristic or attribute. We could assign the value like this:

$X = Happy$

This means we are saying the *name* X is assigned the *value* Happy. We could later tell the computer:

Print X

The computer would then display:

Happy

The things the computer is keeping track of are usually called "variables." This is because the VALUE part of it can change when you tell the computer to change it. The fact that the value can vary is why it's called a "variable" – its value is not permanent or constant.

Now let's look over how problems are solved in programming.

CHAPTER SEVEN: ALGORITHMS

"Algorithm" is a mathematical term that means a plan for solving a problem. It consists of a sequence of steps to solve a problem or perform an action.

Computers use algorithms. An algorithm is a set of instructions that is used to get something done.

For example, an algorithm for selecting the right kind of shirt might have the following steps:

1. Pick a shirt from your closet.
2. Put the shirt on.
3. Look at yourself in the mirror.
4. If you like it, go to step 6.
5. If you don't like it, return to step 2.
6. End of procedure.

Computers perform functions by processing algorithms. You can create algorithms for computers to follow that other people can then use in the future without having to write out the entire list of steps again.

For example, when your computer prints something, there are many massive algorithms it uses to figure out which type of printer you have, how to convey the document to the printer in a way it understands, etc. This is all taken care of in the background so that all you need to do is click "print." These algorithms were written by others to get the computer and printer to comply with your wishes.

Another example of an algorithm could be a simple recipe, such as:

1. Crack three eggs and pour their contents into a small bowl – attempt to avoid getting eggshell in the bowl.
2. In the case of eggshells, remove any eggshells from the bowl.
3. Beat the 3 eggs for 90 seconds in the small bowl.
4. Put a small frying pan on the stove and turn the burner on to medium temperature.
5. Pour the eggs in a small frying pan and cook until very little to no wetness remains.
6. Serve the eggs.

While there are similarities, computers and people do not use algorithms in the same way; there are similar features between real life algorithms and computer algorithms, but they are not identical.

Computers can't think – they operate in a completely literal manner – so when writing an algorithm for computers, there are certain characteristics that must be present for a computer to use the algorithm. People can deduce things and extrapolate data; people have imagination. Computers can only do what they've been told to do.

To fully understand what an algorithm is for computers, some terms and concepts must be cleared up first. Algorithms are composed of five separate characteristics:

1. Result: the outcome of something.

2. Finite amount of time: an exact amount of time for something.

3. Well-ordered: listed out in the correct sequence and in an organized fashion.

4. Effectively computable operations: this refers to a command that can be processed successfully by a computer.

5. Unambiguous: ambiguous means unclear, confusing, not specified. Un = not. Something that is unambiguous means that it is clear and defined.

Let's go over each of these points in detail.

RESULT

Result: the outcome of something.

In computers, a response could be considered the result. You type in: "Tell me the date," the computer replies: "Jan 3, 2022." "Jan 3, 2022" would be the result. Answers to problems are also considered a result.

Algorithms always have a result. If there is no result, it cannot be considered a valid algorithm.

For example: print the number "2," Result: 2.

FINITE AMOUNT OF TIME

Finite amount of time: an exact amount of time for something.

Algorithms should have a finite number of operations included in them and should execute these operations in a set period of time. Algorithms should never be open-ended or infinite. Since each step of an algorithm takes a certain amount of time to be completed, this would mean the algorithm would be completed in a finite amount of time.

An incorrect algorithm would be:

1. Start at an amount of 1
2. Add 1 to that amount
3. Go to step 2

The computer would then count 0, 1, 2, 3, 4, etc. forever.

For example, "Count from 1 to 10, then print a message that says, 'I counted from 1-10'," would be a correct algorithm because it contains a finite amount of steps.

WELL-ORDERED

Well-ordered: listed out in the correct sequence and in an organized fashion. Computers can only execute an algorithm if it is well-ordered. If it is put out of sequence or no sequence is specified, etc., the computer cannot process the algorithm.

For example, this is an incorrect algorithm because it is not well-ordered:

1. Close the program
2. Print "I am here" inside the program
3. Save your work in the program
4. Open the program

EFFECTIVELY COMPUTABLE OPERATIONS

Effectively computable operations: this refers to a command that can be processed successfully by a computer. The phrase literally means an operation that can be computed in an effective way.

In algorithms, all of the parts of the algorithm must be possible to execute.

For example, a non-effectively computable operation could be: "multiply green by red" – the computer can't process this because it isn't computable. Operations contained in algorithms must be effectively computable operations, such as, "2 + 2 =."

UNAMBIGUOUS

Unambiguous: ambiguous means unclear, confusing, not specified. Un = not. Something that is unambiguous means that it is clear and defined.

In computers, your algorithms must be unambiguous. You have to be extremely specific about each step/part of an algorithm or the algorithms cannot be processed by the computer.

For example, if you have an algorithm that is processing a list of ten numbers, then a step of your algorithm is "delete the number," the computer cannot process this because you did not clearly specify which number you wanted deleted.

Now that you know the above terms and concepts, we have the full definition of "algorithm" as defined in the book *Invitation to Computer Science* by American authors Schneider and Gersting:

Algorithm: *A well-ordered collection of unambiguous and effectively computable operations that when executed produces a result and halts in a finite amount of time.*

Sorting means to put items in an exact sequence or order. Computers sort items often. On your computer, you can sort files by when they were created, their name, etc. Algorithms can be used by computers to organize data.

For example, you can sort files on your computer by name or date. This is done by a sorting algorithm within the computer. There are several different ways algorithms can be written to sort data.

In learning how to program, you would write algorithms to perform various functions. Computers have many algorithms programmed into them already that cause them to do a lot of the actions you use computers for. For example, your computer performs many complicated steps to save a document on your computer. These steps are taken care of because programmers entered in algorithms to handle it for you.

Whether or not you ever learn to write code, it is helpful to know the elements that make up a program, which we will now cover.

CHAPTER EIGHT: FIVE ELEMENTS OF A PROGRAM

There are five key elements to any computer program:

1. Entrance
2. Control/Branching (decision points within a program)
3. Variables
4. Subprograms (programs within programs)
5. Exit

Let's go over each of these in detail.

ENTRANCE

A computer is a simple machine when you get down to it. It can only do one thing at a time, and it performs a computer program's instructions in the exact order in which the computer programmer puts them. It can only execute (perform or run) an instruction if it is directed to.

This means that any computer program has to have a clearly marked "first instruction." This is the first task that the computer will perform when the computer program is started. From that point forward, each instruction in the program will direct the computer what instruction to perform next after it performs the current instruction.

There are different ways to specify the entrance point, depending on which computer programming language is being used, but every computer program has a defined entrance point.

CONTROL/BRANCHING

Computers are often used to automate actions that would otherwise be performed by people. One of the most common things a person will be asked to do in performing a job is to assess the condition of a thing and, based on the condition of that thing, choose between two or more possible courses of action. In other words, they will have to make a decision. An example would be the activity of "a teacher grading a stack of papers":

1. Take the next student paper from the top of the stack.
2. Grade the paper.
3. Write the grade on the paper.
4. If the grade is 70% or higher, put the paper in a "Passed" stack.
5. If the grade is below 70%, put the paper in a "Failed" stack.

You can see that there are two possible "paths" here. A path is "a possible course of action arising from a decision." Think of it as what happens when you come to a fork in the road. You have to decide on a course of action – which road do you take? This is also called a branch.

All but the simplest of computer programs will need to do the same thing. That is, they will have to check the condition of a piece of data, and based on the condition of that data, they will have to execute different sets of computer instructions.

In order to do this, the program will make use of special computer instructions called "control" instructions. These are just instructions that tell the computer what to look at in making a decision, and then tell the computer what to do for each possible decision. The most fundamental control statement for a computer is "if." It is used like this:

IF [condition to check checked] THEN [branch of computer instructions to execute]

Here, the "IF" is the control statement; the "THEN" is the branching instruction that points to the path of the program to execute if the control statement is true.

VARIABLES

We covered variables earlier and they are a key part of programs.

As a recap, a variable is a piece of data that a computer program uses to keep track of values that can change as the program is executed. This might be something like "the grade of the student paper that was just graded" or "the color of paint to use for the next car on the assembly line."

Variables are a vital part of any computer program because they make it so a computer program can be used for more than a single, predetermined set of values. You can imagine that if "the color of paint to use for the next car on the "assembly line" was only ever able to be "blue," the computer program using that data wouldn't be very useful. It would make a lot more sense to make it so the computer program could change that value for each car that was going to be painted.

When you are writing variables in a computer program, they usually are written in a manner like this:

[name of the variable] = [value of the variable]

For example, you might have something like this:

color = "red"

Here, the variable is named "color," and the value of that variable has been set to "red." In other words, the variable named "color" is now "equal" to the word "red."

Let's look at the example of "a teacher grading a stack of papers." Here, we could have a variable called "Paper Grade" that changed each time the teacher graded a paper. You could also have variables for the total number of questions on the paper ("Total Questions") for both the number of questions the student answered correctly ("Correct Questions") and for the grade of the paper.

The written description from above:

1. Take the next student paper from the top of the "To Be Graded" stack.
2. Grade the paper.
3. Write the grade on the paper.
4. If the grade is 70% or higher, put the paper in a "Passed" stack.
5. If the grade is below 70%, put the paper in a "Failed" stack.

In computer language, the procedure might look something like this:

1. Retrieve Next Paper
2. Set Total Questions = [total questions in current Paper]
3. Grade Paper
4. Set Correct Questions = [number of questions answered correctly]
5. Set Paper Grade = [Correct Questions/Total Questions]
6. If (Paper Grade >= 70%) then Paper Status = "passed"
7. (Paper Grade < 70%) then Paper Status = "failed"

This is a simple computer program.

As a note, the >= (greater-than sign followed by equal sign) is a symbol used to show that a comparison should be made. Specifically, this "greater-than or equal" symbol is an instruction to check whether the data on the left side of the symbol is more than or equal in amount or quantity to the data on the right side. The answer to this comparison is an answer of "true" or "false."

For example: 5 >= 4

This means "check whether 5 is greater than or equal to 4." Since five is in fact greater than four, the answer is "true."
Another example: 3 >= 6

This means "check whether 3 is greater than or equal to 6." The answer is "false."

As a final example: 6 >= 6

This means "check whether 6 is greater than or equal to 6." The answer is "true."

The reverse (opposite) symbol of >= is <=, which checks for whether the data on the left side of the symbol is *lesser/fewer* or *equal* to the data on the right side.

Each time the computer runs the seven-step procedure listed earlier, it could have different values for each of the variables in the program, depending on how many questions the paper being graded has and how many of those questions the student answered correctly.

For example, let's say the paper has 100 questions, and the student answers 82 of them correctly. After the program is run, the result would be the following:

Total Questions: 100
Correct Questions: 82
Paper Grade: 82%
Paper Status: Passed

As another example, let's say the paper has 50 questions, and the student answers 30 of them correctly. After the program is run, the result would be the following:

Total Questions: 50
Correct Questions: 30
Paper Grade: 60%
Paper Status: Failed

To clarify the need for variables: Let's say that at the time this computer program was being created, all papers at the school had 100 questions, and the teachers told the programmer to make it so that the number of questions was always assumed to be 100. In that case, the programmer wouldn't use a variable called "Total Questions."

Instead, she could make the program look like this:

1. Retrieve Next Paper
2. Grade Paper
3. Set Correct Questions = [number of questions answered correctly]
4. Set Paper Grade = [Correct Questions/100]
5. If (Paper Grade >= 70%) then Paper Status = "passed"
6. If (Paper Grade < 70%) then Paper Status = "failed"

Notice that on line 4 of the program, the programmer set the number of questions to 100.

Now, let's say that the school introduces the concept of "quizzes," which are smaller papers with only 20 questions. If the paper being handled by the computer program is a quiz, the grade will no longer be accurate – even if a student got all 20 questions correct, he/she would only get a grade of 20% (20/100).

A good programmer will analyze the need that the program is meant to resolve, then build the program so that it can handle changing aspects of that need over time.

Another valuable control statement is a loop. This is where part of the program is executed over and over until a certain condition is met.

In real-world terms, an example might be "grade papers one at a time until all the papers have been graded" or "make five copies of this document."

In a computer program, a loop would look something like this:

- [start loop]
  o Perform action
  o If [end condition has been met] then [exit the loop]
  o If [end condition has not been met] then [repeat the loop]
- [end loop]

The program we looked at that grades papers could be set up as a loop. The instructions would be laid out like this:

- [start loop]
  o Take the next student paper from the top of the "To Be Graded" stack.
  o Grade the paper.
  o Write the grade on the paper.
  o If the grade is 70% or higher, put the paper in a "Passed" stack.
  o If the grade is below 70%, put the paper in a "Failed" stack.
  o If there are no more papers in the "To Be Graded" stack, exit the loop.
  o If there are more papers in the "To Be Graded" stack, repeat the loop.
- [end loop]

Often loops make use of a special variable called a "counter." The counter keeps track of how many times the loop has been executed. This can be used to make sure the loop is only executed when needed.

Let's add a counter to the grading program we're looking at as well as two new variables: "Total Papers" will be used to hold the value "how many papers need to be graded," while "Counter" will be used to hold the value "how many times the loop has been executed."

1. Set Total Papers = [total papers to be graded]

2. Set Counter = 0

3. If (Counter < Total Papers):

   a. Retrieve next Paper
   b. Set Total Questions = [total questions in current Paper]
   c. Grade paper
   d. Set Correct Questions = [number of questions answered correctly]
   e. Set Paper Grade = [Correct Questions/Total Questions]
   f. If (Paper Grade >= 70%) then Paper Status = "passed"
   g. If (Paper Grade < 70%) then Paper Status = "failed"
   h. Counter = Counter + 1
   i. Go to step 3

4. [Continue on with the rest of the program]

Here, the loop is found in step 3.

Let's break down what each step is doing here:

Step 1:   Count how many papers are in the "to be graded" stack and set the value of the "Total Papers"

38

variable to that number.

Step 2: Create a variable called "Counter" and set it to the value zero. This variable will be used to keep track of how many papers are graded.

Step 3: Use the control statement "if" to see if we should execute a loop.

Step 3a–3g: Grade the paper; this has been covered above.

Step 3h: Since we have now graded a paper, add one to our Counter variable.

Step 3i: Go to the top of the loop, where we check to see if we need to execute the loop all over again.

Let's see what would happen if we used this program to grade two papers. Let's say that the papers look like this:

Paper 1:
Total questions on the paper: 100
Total questions that were answered correctly: 95

Paper 2:
Total questions on the paper: 20
Total questions that were answered correctly: 10

If we analyze what happens when the program is executed by the computer, it would look like this:

Total Papers = 2
Counter = 0
0 is less than 2, so loop will be executed
Paper 1 Retrieved
Total Questions = 100
Paper 1 Graded

Correct Questions = 95
Paper Grade = 95%
Paper Status = "passed"
Counter = 1
1 is less than 2, so loop will be executed
Paper 2 Retrieved
Total Questions = 20
Paper 1 Graded
Correct Questions = 10
Paper Grade = 50%
Paper Status = "failed"
Counter = 2
2 is not less than 2, so loop will not be executed
[Continue on with the rest of the program]

SUBPROGRAMS

As covered earlier, computer programs are generally executed in order, from the start point to the end point. This is called the "path of execution."

The main series of instructions in a program is called the "main program."

It is sometimes valuable to create another program that can be used by the main program as needed. This is called a subprogram. It is no different from any other program – it is made up of the same elements (entrance point, variables, control and branching statements, and exit point). However, a subprogram isn't used all by itself. Instead, the main program can execute the subprogram as needed. Here, the main program stops executing, and the subprogram starts executing. When the subprogram is done executing, the main program continues on where it left off.

This is referred to as "calling" the subprogram – that is, the main program calls the subprogram, the subprogram starts and stops, and the main program continues on where it left off before calling the subprogram.

This is useful in creating programs because the computer programmer doesn't have to enter the instructions of the subprogram over and over. You only type them in once, and then when you need that subprogram to be called by the main program, you only have to type in one instruction – the instruction to call the subprogram. This lets you reuse the instructions you entered in for the subprogram rather than rewriting them.

EXIT

Every program must have an instruction that tells the computer that the program is no longer running. Much like the Entrance, the exact instruction for this varies based on the computer language used, but all computer languages will have this type of instruction.

SUMMARY

The fundamental elements of any computer program are:

1) An entrance point – the first instruction to be performed.

2) Control and branching statements – to control what is done and in what order.

3) Variables – changeable items, held in computer memory, for the program to use as it operates.

4) Subprograms – repeatable sets of computer instructions that act like mini-programs. The main program can use them as needed.

5) An exit point – the last instruction to be completed, so the computer knows the program isn't operating anymore.

Now you know the elements that make up computer programs. Well done!

This book covers the programming language Small Basic. So, let's discuss what that is exactly.

CHAPTER NINE: SMALL BASIC

Small Basic is a programming language released by Microsoft in 2011. Small Basic includes an Integrated Development Environment (IDE – a tool in which one writes their code) and libraries (sets of pre-manufactured code for use). It can be used to write basic programs and games.

The .NET Framework is a collection of tools and pre-made software that helps software developers to make computer programs. It was created by Microsoft and has several programming languages that it can work with. As a developer, you can write a program that uses one or more of these languages. The .NET Framework can take these programs and convert them down to instructions that will work on pretty much any computer that is compatible with (able to work with) this .NET Framework. This means you only have to write the program once, and not have to write variations of it for all the various types of computers you'd like to have run the program.

Small Basic is based on .NET and so familiarizing yourself with Small Basic makes it easier to learn other .NET programming languages, such as C# (a popular programming language from Microsoft), in the future. This book is the perfect undercut for those interested in learning C# and other .NET technologies.

The purpose of Small Basic is to provide a programming language that is designed to make coding more approachable for newcomers. It is a great learning resource for beginners!

We are getting very close to writing code. In the next chapter, we will cover some tips that will help you through this book.

CHAPTER TEN: CODING TIPS

If you run into any trouble while going through this book, here are some tips:

1)   Ensure you understand all the words and terms being used – clear up any you don't understand.

2)   Ensure your code is written exactly as laid out here. A small error in the code, such as a missing comma, can ruin the whole program. Code must be exact for programs to run properly, so always meticulously check your code for errors.

3)   Research online for solutions.

4)   You can also contact The Tech Academy and ask for assistance – learncodinganywhere.com

CHALLENGES

At the end of some chapters, we will have an "END OF CHAPTER CHALLENGE." These are opportunities for you to put together all that you've studied in that chapter. At times you will also be instructed to figure out solutions to problems on your own. Working software developers are often assigned projects and tasks they've never done before. A key element of the job is researching solutions online. You'll find that some of the challenges in this book will instruct you to do something that we haven't taught you yet. This was done intentionally. We want you to gain experience in locating new data online and figuring out things on your own. In the words of more than one software developer: "I get paid to Google things!"

Some of these challenges will be a repeat of tasks you've already performed. The reasons for this are to:

a. Provide you with an opportunity to create your own approach, and

b. Allow you to better understand and remember code through repetition.

Well done on making it through these beginning chapters! Now we are going to start coding!

CHAPTER ELEVEN: YOUR FIRST ASSIGNMENT

Here is your first task:

Go to smallbasic-publicwebsite.azurewebsites.net and download Small Basic.

Then install it on your computer using all default settings.

Now that Small Basic is installed on your machine:

Open Small Basic.

You should see something similar to this:

This is the IDE (Integrated Development Environment) that you will be using to write your code as you create computer programs.

The white area where you will type your code is called the "code editor" or "Editor" for short.

The top bar, where such options as New, Open, and Save are listed, is called the "Toolbar."

To write code, you simply type text inside the Editor.

SMALL BASIC TERMS

A statement is an instruction given to a computer. Each line of code you write is a statement. Your Small Basic programs will usually be composed of a series of statements.

When you execute a Small Basic program, the computer reads and executes the first statement. After executing the first statement, it moves on to the next statement and executes that, and on from there – line by line.

In Small Basic, an object is a combination of an operation (such as a subprogram) and property (such as a variable). Objects are indicated by a small orange cube that looks like this:

In Small Basic, operations (also referred to as algorithms) are indicated by a small cogwheel icon that looks like this:

Operations are the actions we can take on objects.

The property (also called data) portion of objects are indicated by a painter's palette:

Properties of an object are the various traits or characteristics we can assign to it. For example, we can change the background color of an object by assigning a property. You'll learn more about all of this shortly.

There are many objects you can use in Small Basic – TextWindow is one of them. This is the TextWindow:

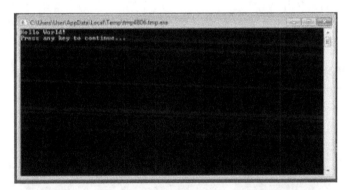

This is also called the Console and is where the result of the program is displayed.

"WriteLine" is an operation that displays text within the TextWindow object.

Parentheses, quotation marks, and periods all perform various functions when writing code and are part of its syntax. For example, in Small Basic, to print text, you must type the desired text within quotation marks ("").

HELLO WORLD

A very common first program that people write when starting out with a programming language is to have the computer display the words: "Hello World."

To do so, type this code in the Editor:

```
TextWindow.WriteLine("Hello World!")
```

You've written your first program using Small Basic! Now, there are two ways to run the program:

1. Click the Run button on the Toolbar, or
2. Press F5 on your keyboard.

Do the following:

Run your program.

If you have created the program correctly, you should see a console window that looks like this:

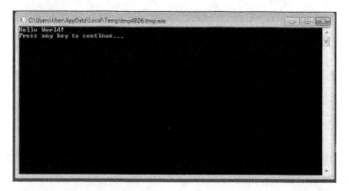

If you didn't get that result, check your work and try again. If you did get that result, good job!

In our code, "Hello World!" is the parameter (data given to an operation for use as the operation is performed) for our WriteLine operation. Operations can either accept one or more parameters, or none at all.

To summarize the program we just wrote: it contains one statement and this statement instructed the computer to display the text "Hello World!"

You should always save your code regularly. After all, you don't want your computer to shut off after you've spent hours writing out code – that will result in losing all your hard work. You can save your code in two ways:

1. Click Save on the Toolbar, or
2. While holding down the Ctrl key on the keyboard, press the S key and then release both keys.

Do the following:

Save your program on your desktop or in a folder of your choosing. Give it any filename you like.

CHAPTER TWELVE: EXPANDING THE PROGRAM

There are properties we can assign to the object TextWindow, that change the color of the text and the background color behind the text – these are ForegroundColor and BackgroundColor respectively.

In the Editor, write and execute this code:

```
TextWindow.WriteLine("Hello World")
TextWindow.BackgroundColor = "White"
TextWindow.ForegroundColor = "Blue"
```

Good job! You've added colors!

In our code, we included the parameters "White" and "Blue" to specify the exact colors.

As a note, you can find the full list of colors for Small Basic here:

blogs.msdn.microsoft.com/smallbasic/2015/06/20/the-hex-colors-in-small-basic/

Feel free to play around with this and change the parameters to other colors such as yellow, red, green, etc.

Note that unlike the WriteLine operation, the properties (BackgroundColor and ForegroundColor) did not need parentheses. Instead, we assigned the values (in these cases, colors) using an equal sign. This is an example of syntax – the arbitrary rules on how to write code in a programming language.

To further demonstrate syntax, do the following:

Delete the quotation marks ("") around an assigned value (one of the colors) and attempt running your program.

You will receive an error message. This is an example of a syntax error. Something as simple as leaving out quotation marks can cause a program not to run!

As we just covered, each color is a parameter (which is, again, the data given to an operation for use as the operation is performed).

And as we discussed earlier, a variable is a symbol used to represent an unknown quantity or a quantity that may change. In computers, a variable is used to store data for later use as the program executes.

The computer usually gives each variable these pieces of data:

1. NAME (also called an identifier), and
2. VALUE.

The NAME is used to identify the exact piece of data, and the VALUE is used to show the actual data we need to keep track of.

Usually, the "=" symbol is used to set the VALUE of a variable.

When the "=" symbol is used to set the value of a variable, it is usually used like this:

[NAME of the variable] = [VALUE that is being assigned to that variable].

For example:

fabricColor = "blue"

Here, there is a piece of data that the computer is keeping track of that has been given the name "fabricColor." By using the "=" symbol, we can set the value of the piece of data called "fabricColor." In this case, we are setting that value to the series of letters "blue."

END OF CHAPTER CHALLENGE

Write a program that contains the following elements:

1. A background color,
2. A foreground color,
3. The Program.Delay() operation, and
4. The WriteLine operation.

Note: You are being asked to use the Program.Delay() operation, which is something you haven't learned in this book. As we mentioned earlier, you will occasionally be tasked with performing actions you haven't been taught yet. This is intentional and is a vital component of the learning process. You will need to research online to define code, and to locate data and solutions. Google is your friend!

CHAPTER THIRTEEN: MORE VARIABLES

Read() is a property that instructs the computer to stand by (wait) for the user to type something and then press the Enter/Return key. After the user types in data and hits Enter/Return, the computer takes what they typed and passes the data to the program.

CONCATENATING A STRING

Concatenate means to connect items together, like links in a chain. It means to take one piece of data and stick it on the end of another piece of data.

A string is data that represents text or a series of text.

For example, concatenating the string "dev" and the string "ices" makes the string "devices."

STORING AND PRINTING VARIABLES

Now let's write a program that can store *and* print variables!

Write and execute this code:

```
TextWindow.Write("What is your favorite food?: ")
food = TextWindow.Read()
TextWindow.WriteLine("Your favorite food is " + food + "! Yummy!")
TextWindow.Write("Which city would you most like to visit?: ")
city = TextWindow.Read()
TextWindow.WriteLine(city + " sounds like a great place to visit!")
```

Well done! You created a basic program. In it, you assigned variables, allowed user input and concatenated strings.

As we recently discussed, a variable is a place where values are stored for later use. In your code, food and city are variables. The text the user types in response to food and city are stored in variables. The variable "food" was used to store the user's favorite food, while the variable "city" was used to store the city that the user wished to visit.

When naming a variable, it is recommended that you use a name that describes the variable.

For example:

```
user_address = TextWindow.Read()
```

would be a good name for a variable that stores a user's address. Whereas:

```
giraffe = TextWindow.Read()
```

would *not* be a good name for storing user address data.

END OF CHAPTER CHALLENGE

Write and execute a program that contains the following elements:

- TextWindow.Write operation,
- TextWindow.Read operation, and
- CursorTop property.

As a note, a cursor is the small vertical bar on your computer screen that flashes – it indicates where to type. In this challenge, you are again being assigned to use code we haven't taught you yet. This will continue in future challenges.

CHAPTER FOURTEEN: MATH AND NUMBERS

You can also store and utilize numbers in variables and perform mathematical equations.

In the Editor, write and execute this code:

```
First_number = 5
Second_number = 10
Third_number = 15
Fourth_number = 20
Fifth_number = 50
Sixth_number = 16
TextWindow.WriteLine(Second_number + Third_number)
```

You just added 10 and 15 together!

The variables were each assigned these values:

- You assigned the variable First_number the value 5
- You assigned the variable Second_number the value 10
- You assigned the variable Third_number the value 15
- You assigned the variable Fourth_number the value 20
- You assigned the variable Fifth_number the value 50
- You assigned the variable Sixth_number the value 16

When we used strings as a parameter earlier (i.e., the statements: What is your favorite food?, Yummy, etc.), we were required to surround the text with quotation marks, but with numeric parameters, quotation marks are unnecessary – yet another example of syntax.

You can also perform subtraction. Add this code beneath your existing code and execute it:

```
TextWindow.WriteLine(25 - First_number)
```

You subtracted 5 from 25 and displayed the result!

You can multiply numbers. Add this code beneath your existing code and execute it:

```
TextWindow.WriteLine(20 * Fourth_number)
```

This should display 400.

You can divide numbers as well. Add this code beneath your existing code and execute it:

```
TextWindow.WriteLine(400 / Fifth_number)
```

This results in 8!

We can also get the square root of a number but to do so, we have to import (bring in) the Math library.

A "library" is a pre-made package of computer code. Libraries are useful in computer programming because it means the programmer doesn't have to write the code to do the functions that the library provides; he or she can just use the pre-made library. The Math library contains additional mathematical operations that can be added to Small Basic – for example, it allows you to use the SquareRoot operation.

Add this code beneath your existing code and execute it:

```
TextWindow.WriteLine(Math.SquareRoot(Sixth_number))
```

You found the square root of 16.

Using the Math library, you can also round numbers. Add this code beneath your existing code and execute it:

```
TextWindow.WriteLine(Math.Round(5.6))
```

You rounded 5 up to 6!

Feel free to change your variables and perform your own math operations!

TEMPERATURE

Another interesting thing you can do with Small Basic is – convert temperature from Fahrenheit to Celsius.

The way you convert Fahrenheit to Celsius is: Fahrenheit temperature minus 32, multiplied by 5/9ths

Or written as an equation:
$$T_{(°C)} = (T_{(°F)} - 32) \times 5/9$$

For the purposes of this book, it is not necessary for you to understand this equation.

In the Editor, write and execute this code:

```
TextWindow.Write("What is the temperature in Fahrenheit? ")
Fahrenheit = TextWindow.ReadNumber()
Celsius = (Fahrenheit - 32) * 5/9
TextWindow.WriteLine("The temperature in Celsius is: " + Celsius)
```

Could you see how this might be a useful program?

We can also write a short program that randomly provides the user with a number.

Write and execute this code:

```
TextWindow.WriteLine(Math.GetRandomNumber(100))
```

END OF CHAPTER CHALLENGE

Write a program that includes the following:

- The TextWindow.Title property,
- Assigning a value to a variable,
- The TextWindow.WriteLine operation, and
- The TextWindow.Top property.

CHAPTER FIFTEEN: CONDITIONAL STATEMENTS

A condition is something that other things depend on. In math, a condition is something that is required for something else to be true. Conditions are points that must be present for other points to be present. If you say something is "conditional," that means it relies on the state of another thing.

For example, the statement "Electricity is allowed to flow through this part of the computer if you type 1" could be a condition. Or say you have a word problem like this: "Come up with two digits that, when added together, equal six – but the digits 2 and 4 are never to be used to get the answer." Here, the part that tells you that you can't use the numbers 2 or 4 in your answer is a condition.

A conditional statement takes place when you tell the computer: depending upon_____, do_____. An "If Statement" is a type of conditional statement that means: if this, then that.

As was covered earlier, a branch is a point of decision. Branches are a fundamental element of how we make computers do useful work. A branch instruction tells the computer to go to somewhere other than the primary series of instructions and instead execute an alternate series of instructions; usually based on some decision the computer has to make. It is a statement written in the program's code to make the computer shift from one area to another.

In order to tell the computer how to analyze conditional statements, you'll make use of comparison instructions such as the < and > symbols. < means "lesser than" and > means "greater than."

The EndIf statement tells the computer that we are done with an operation.

Write and execute this code:

```
If(5 < 10) Then
  TextWindow.WriteLine("Five is less than ten.")
EndIf
```

Well done! Since it is true that 5 is less than 10, the program ended.

END OF CHAPTER CHALLENGE

Complete the following:

Write and execute your own conditional statement.

CHAPTER SIXTEEN: MORE CONDITIONAL STATEMENTS

In Small Basic, start is called a label. It's similar to a bookmark within your program. In this case, the start label defines the beginning of our code and gives us a place to return to in our program.

Goto is an instruction which makes the program go to an exact place in the series of instructions that make up the program. "Goto" statements utilize labels and redirect the program to a label.

Now let's try using an ElseIf Statement, which is basically a second If Statement and gives us another option to choose from. We will also use an Else Statement that tells the computer, "Otherwise, do_____." You'll get a better idea of this through trying it out.

Write and execute this code:

```
start:
TextWindow.Write("Are you a vegan? ")
Vegan = TextWindow.Read()
If Vegan = "Yes" Then
  TextWindow.WriteLine("I know, you've told me already. Several times...")
ElseIf Vegan = "No" Then
  TextWindow.WriteLine("Looks like meat is back on the menu!")
Else
  TextWindow.WriteLine("Please enter Yes or No.")
  Goto start
EndIf
```

You just created a program that has different outcomes based on the user's answer. Pretty cool!

Clock.Hour is a built-in instruction in Small Basic that gives the time on your computer.

Using Clock.Hour, let's create a program that can tell the difference between a.m. and p.m.

Write and execute this code:

```
If (Clock.Hour < 12) Then
  TextWindow.WriteLine("It is a.m.")
ElseIf (Clock.Hour >= 12) Then
  TextWindow.WriteLine("It is p.m.")
EndIf
```

It tells you if it's a.m. or p.m.!

There is also another way you can write this code. Write and execute this code:

```
If (Clock.Hour < 12) Then
  TextWindow.WriteLine("It is a.m.")
Else
  TextWindow.WriteLine("It is p.m.")
EndIf
```

This code has the same output as our previous program.

We can use conditional statements to greet people depending on the time of the day. Write and execute this code:

```
If (Clock.Hour < 12) Then
  TextWindow.WriteLine("Good morning!")
ElseIf (Clock.Hour <= 18) Then
  TextWindow.WriteLine("Good afternoon!")
Else
  TextWindow.WriteLine("Good evening!")
EndIf
```

Did your program greet you correctly?

As you can see, the code is sometimes automatically indented for you. This is so that the code is sectioned off and you can easily read through it. In Small Basic, this indentation isn't required, and the program will run whether or not the code is indented.

In math, a "remainder" is the number left over after dividing numbers. For example, 7 divided by 2 is 3, with a remainder of 1.

Math.Remainder is an operation in Small Basic that divides the first number by the second and returns (gives back) the remainder. E.g., all even numbers will have a 0 remainder when divided by 2 (nothing left over – they divide evenly).

Now let's use some of what we've learned so far (and learn some more) to build a program that will round numbers and tell us whether the numbers are odd or even.

Write and execute this code:

```
TextWindow.Write("Type a number that includes a decimal: ")
Number = TextWindow.ReadNumber()
TextWindow.Write("Now we will round your number! ...")
TextWindow.Write("Your rounded number is: " + Math.Round(Number) + ".")
Remainder = Math.Remainder(Math.Round(Number), 2)
If (Remainder = 0) Then
  TextWindow.WriteLine(" This number is even!")
Else
    TextWindow.WriteLine(" This is an odd number!")
EndIf
```

Did you notice how the text all just blurted out at once? Let's add a delay so that one sentence displays at a time. To do so, we use the Program.Delay() operation that you learned about during a previous challenge. Within the parentheses after "Delay," you enter how many milliseconds you want to wait before the program continues.

Let's dissect Program.Delay():

1)   Program is the *object* (an item that has operations and/or properties),
2)   Delay is the *operation*, and
3)   The milliseconds are the *parameters*. As a reminder, parameters are data given to an operation for use as the operation is performed.

Write and execute this code:

```
TextWindow.Write("Type a number that includes a decimal: ")
Number = TextWindow.ReadNumber()
Program.Delay(1000)
TextWindow.Write("Now we will round your number! ...")
Program.Delay(1000)
TextWindow.Write("Your rounded number is: " + Math.Round(Number) + ".")
Program.Delay(1000)
Remainder = Math.Remainder(Math.Round(Number), 2)
If (Remainder = 0) Then
  TextWindow.WriteLine(" This number is even!")
  Program.Delay(1000)
Else
  TextWindow.WriteLine(" This is an odd number!")
  Program.Delay(1000)
EndIf
```

Now the program displays smoothly.

In this program, the If Statement and the Else Statement are control statements. As a reminder, a control statement is instructions that tell the computer what to look at in making a decision, and then tell the computer what to do for each possible decision.

The code that is executed in response to those control statements are the branches (statements written in the program's code to make the computer shift from one area to another).

In our program, the first branch is:

```
TextWindow.WriteLine(" This number is even!")
Program.Delay(1000)
```

And the second branch is:

```
TextWindow.WriteLine(" This is an odd number!")
Program.Delay(1000)
```

END OF CHAPTER CHALLENGE

Write a program that includes the following:

- If statement,
- ElseIf statement,
- Else statement,
- Program.delay,
- Math.Remainder, and
- Math.Ceiling(number).

CHAPTER SEVENTEEN: LOOPS

As we covered earlier, a loop is something that connects back to the beginning point. In computers, a loop is a sequence of instructions that are continually repeated until an exact condition is achieved.

Usually, a loop will occur when a certain set of actions is performed by a computer program. The program would then check to see if it has reached the condition required for completion. If not, it starts over and repeats the set of actions. If so, it exits the loop and moves on to the next consecutive instruction in the computer program.

WHILE LOOPS

A "While Loop" is basically a repeating "if statement." Meaning, you are telling the computer to execute certain code repeatedly *while* a particular condition is present (true) – e.g., while hungry, eat.

Write and execute this code in the text Editor:

```
Amount = 1
While(Amount < 1025)
   TextWindow.WriteLine(Amount)
   Amount = Amount * 2
EndWhile
```

Here, we are telling the program, "As long as the variable (Amount) is less than 1025, multiply the Amount by 2."

ITERATION

An important aspect of how loops work is the concept of an iteration.

To iterate means to say or do something again; to repeat something. Iteration is the act of repeating. Iteration means to go through a defined series of actions, repeating a certain number of times. Usually, this defined series of actions is repeated a certain number of times or until a condition is met.

In this diagram of a basic loop, an iteration would consist of one time through the loop (whether to completion or a repeat):

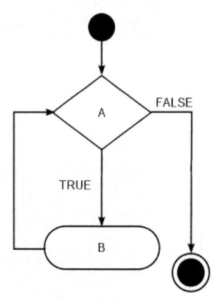

Computer programs are usually created in iterations: Coming up with a basic working version, reviewing the program for mistakes to correct and improvements to make, doing that work, and repeating. This can be continued indefinitely.

FOR LOOPS

A "For Loop" is used to repeat a section of code a number of times. For Loops are used when the number of iterations is known.

Here's an example:

for each student in the class (25), provide a grade

Write and execute this For Loop:

```
For B = 1 To 10
  TextWindow.WriteLine(B)
EndFor
```

In our code, we assign the values 1 through 10 to the variable B one at a time as the loop is executed. An integer is a whole number (such as 3 or 5). An increment is a distinct increase in amount. Incrementing is to distinctly increase a number. "1 To 10" above was incrementing an integer. But since we assigned a variable ("B"), we were technically "incrementing a variable." And so, we utilized a For Loop to increment (count up) a variable.

If we create a loop and don't close the loop, the code will continue on forever. This is called an infinite loop.

Write and execute this code:

```
Begin:
A = 50
If A > 25 Then
  TextWindow.WriteLine("50 is more than 25!")
  Goto Begin
EndIf
```

You will see that when this program is executed, the computer just continues to print "50 is more than 25!" on the screen until you close the window. This is because the condition statement in your loop ("If A > 25") is always true, so the loop always returns to the beginning and does another iteration. Under certain circumstances, an infinite loop can lock up a computer and require the shutdown and restart of the computer in order to stop the loop.

To close the loop in our example, you would simply get rid of the "Begin:" label and the "Goto" statement. Do so and re-run your code.

In Small Basic, "Step" can be used to count up, so let's now make a program – using a For Loop – that counts out only even numbers up to 30.

Write and execute this code:

```
For B = 2 To 30 Step 2
  TextWindow.WriteLine(B)
EndFor
```

So now, let's reverse the countdown and use only odd numbers!

Write and execute this code:

```
For B = 29 To 1 Step -2
  TextWindow.WriteLine(B)
EndFor
```

It's interesting to note that every loop can be translated into a conditional statement. For example, we can rewrite our last For Loop as a conditional statement.

Write and execute this code:

```
B = 29
start:
TextWindow.WriteLine(B)
B = B - 2
If (0 < B) Then
  Goto start
EndIf
```

Actually, here's a fun fact: Every time you write a While Loop in your code, the computer automatically converts it to an If Statement with one or more Goto Statements. This is done behind the scenes; you won't see a change in the actual instructions you typed in the editor.

Let's do a loop that will find out the larger of two numbers.

Write and execute this code:

```
TextWindow.Write("Type in a number: ")
First_Number = TextWindow.ReadNumber()
TextWindow.Write("Type in another number: ")
Second_Number = TextWindow.ReadNumber()
If (First_Number > Second_Number) Then
  Larger = First_Number
Else
  Larger = Second_Number
EndIf
TextWindow.WriteLine("The larger number is: " + Larger)
```

Well done! You made another basic program.

END OF CHAPTER CHALLENGE 1

Write a program that includes the following:

- A For Loop, and
- A While Loop.

END OF CHAPTER CHALLENGE 2

Write a program that includes the following:

- Create a loop that counts numbers backward, one number at a time, starting at 100 down to 1, that also includes

```
Program.Delay(100).
```

CHAPTER EIGHTEEN: GRAPHICS WINDOW

You can customize certain aspects of the Text Window and how it displays. We touched upon this earlier with foreground color and background color.

There is also a graphics window. Graphics are pictures displayed on a computer.

Like the Text Window that displays text, Small Basic also has a Graphics Window for graphics.

Enter and execute this code:

```
GraphicsWindow.Show()
```

You should see this:

<u>PIXELS</u>

A pixel is the smallest single component of a digital image. It can be thought of as a small dot that helps to make up an image on a computer display, television or similar display device. Each pixel gets set to display a specific color and when many pixels are arranged together, an overall image is displayed that is a composite of the individual pixels.

If you are looking at a picture on a computer, that image is actually made up of many small pixels of different colors. Together, they combine to form the picture.

When you can see the individual dots on a screen, this is referred to as "pixelated". If we zoom in on this deer's ear, the ear is pixelated (meaning, the pixels are visible):

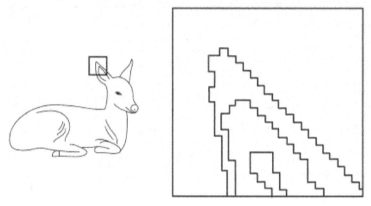

Computer programmers can direct computers where to display pixels on a screen. For example, in a popular language used to create websites, the command pxl (short for pixels) can be used to instruct how large text should be displayed. For example, this code:

font-size: 30px;

would display text of this size:

This is 30px text.

CUSTOMIZING THE GRAPHICS WINDOW

Now, to change the design of the Graphics Window, there are some things you can do – such as using the Height, Width, BackgroundColor and Title properties to customize it.

Write and execute this code:

```
GraphicsWindow.Height = 500
GraphicsWindow.Width = 700
GraphicsWindow.BackgroundColor = "Silver"
GraphicsWindow.Title = "This is the Graphics Window!")
GraphicsWindow.Show()
```

See what that did?

As a note, the numbers in your code specify how many pixels high and how many pixels wide the Graphics Window is.

DRAWING LINES

One of the cool things about the Graphics Window is the ability to draw lines.

To do so, we must specify the X and Y Coordinates. The X Coordinate refers to how far left to right (horizontally) something extends on a grid or a map. The Y Coordinate refers to how far top to bottom (vertically) something extends.

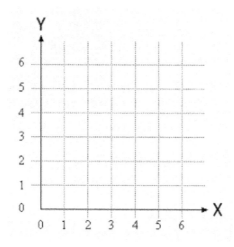

Write and execute this code:

```
GraphicsWindow.DrawLine(10,10,200,10)
GraphicsWindow.DrawLine(10,10,10,200)
GraphicsWindow.DrawLine(10,200,200,200)
GraphicsWindow.DrawLine(200,10,200,200)
```

Now let's walk through the numbers used in our code:

- The first number tells the computer how far left or right the line will be started (called the X Coordinate).
- The second number tells us where the line starts – up and down – (called the Y Coordinate).
- The third number tells the computer where the bottom of the line ends right to left.
- The fourth number tells the computer where the bottom of the line (up and down) ends up.

Each line of your code drew one side of a square!

CHALLENGE

Let's try a challenge now. Accomplish the following:

Draw an X shape using GraphicsWindow.DrawLine

We can also change the color and thickness of a line, by using the PenColor and PenWidth properties respectively.

Write and execute this code:

```
GraphicsWindow.Height = 500
GraphicsWindow.Width = 500
GraphicsWindow.BackgroundColor = "Silver"
GraphicsWindow.Title = "The Colored Square!"
GraphicsWindow.DrawLine(10,10,450,10)
GraphicsWindow.PenWidth = 10
GraphicsWindow.PenColor = "Red"
GraphicsWindow.DrawLine(10,10,10,450)
GraphicsWindow.PenWidth = 20
GraphicsWindow.PenColor = "Blue"
GraphicsWindow.DrawLine(10,450,450,450)
GraphicsWindow.PenWidth = 30
GraphicsWindow.PenColor = "Yellow"
GraphicsWindow.DrawLine(450,10,450,450)
GraphicsWindow.PenWidth = 40
GraphicsWindow.PenColor = "Green"
```

You've displayed lines of various sizes and colors!

LOOPS AND THE GRAPHICS BOX

We can also utilize loops with the Graphics Box.

Write and execute this code:

```
GraphicsWindow.Title = "Growing Lines!"
GraphicsWindow.Height = 500
GraphicsWindow.Width = 500
GraphicsWindow.PenColor = "Red"
GraphicsWindow.BackgroundColor = "Blue"
For A = 1 To 15
  GraphicsWindow.PenWidth = A
  GraphicsWindow.DrawLine(20, A * 20, 400, A * 20)
EndFor
```

Read through your code, can you tell what it's doing?

As you can see by the output, we used a For Loop to gradually increase the thickness of the lines.

DRAWING PIXELS

We can also draw pixels in the Graphics Window.

Write and execute this code:

```
GraphicsWindow.SetPixel(20, 20, "Black")
```

If you can see it, there's a tiny black dot on the screen. That is a pixel and the numbers give the X and Y coordinate for it!

TEXT IN THE GRAPHICS WINDOW

In case you were wondering, we can also add text to the Graphics Window.

Write and execute this code:

```
GraphicsWindow.DrawBoundText(70, 70, 150, "John")
GraphicsWindow.DrawBoundText(120, 70, 150, "Sally")
GraphicsWindow.DrawBoundText(180, 70, 150, "Bill")
GraphicsWindow.DrawBoundText(250, 70, 150, "Jessica")
GraphicsWindow.DrawBoundText(70, 120, 150, "John")
GraphicsWindow.DrawBoundText(120, 120, 150, "Sally")
GraphicsWindow.DrawBoundText(180, 120, 150, "Bill")
GraphicsWindow.DrawBoundText(250, 120, 150, "Jessica")
```

Why are there three sets of numbers? Well, the first number gives the X Coordinate, the second number gives the Y Coordinate, and the third number gives the size of the font.

END OF CHAPTER CHALLENGE

Write a program that includes the following:

- GraphicsWindow.Height,
- GraphicsWindow.Width,
- GraphicsWindow.DrawLine,
- GraphicsWindow.PenWidth,
- GraphicsWindow.PenColor,
- GraphicsWindow.SetPixel,
- GraphicsWindow.DrawBoundText with multiple font sizes, and
- GraphicsWindow.FontItalic.

CHAPTER NINETEEN: SHAPES

Window. We can also paint and create shapes in the Graphics Window.

For a triangle, we need six numbers. The first two indicate where the top of the triangle is placed (left to right, up to down). The second two indicate the left-hand corner, and the third set indicates the right-hand corner.

Write and execute this code:

```
GraphicsWindow.BrushColor = "Green"
GraphicsWindow.FillTriangle(300,150,150,300,450,300)
```

You made a triangle. Good job!

You can also draw and paint squares, rectangles, and ellipses (ovals).

DRAWING CIRCLES

To draw a circle, you use the DrawEllipse operation.

Write and execute this code:

```
GraphicsWindow.Width = 300
GraphicsWindow.Height = 300
GraphicsWindow.BackgroundColor = "Black"
GraphicsWindow.PenColor = "Yellow"
GraphicsWindow.PenWidth = 20
GraphicsWindow.DrawEllipse(50, 50, 200, 200)
```

DRAWING A SUN

To fill a shape with a color, we use the BrushColor property (which specifies the color) and the FillEllipse (which instructs the computer to insert the color inside the circle).

Write and execute this code:

```
GraphicsWindow.Width = 300
GraphicsWindow.Height = 300
GraphicsWindow.BackgroundColor = "Black"
GraphicsWindow.BrushColor = "Yellow"
GraphicsWindow.FillEllipse(50, 50, 200, 200)
```

Good job! You made a sun.

CREATING A CIRCLE WITH VARIABLES

Now let's make a circle using variables.

Write and execute this code:

```
A = 20
B = 50
GraphicsWindow.FillEllipse(A, B, 350, 350)
```

Do you see how that works?
ANIMATING SHAPES

You can also animate shapes and move them around using the Animate() operation. The first thing we must include in the parentheses is the name of the shape, followed by x coordinate, y coordinate, and then the speed of the move.

Write and execute this code:

```
Triangle = Shapes.AddTriangle(50, 100, 100, 50, 150, 100)
Program.Delay(1000)
Shapes.Animate(Triangle, 200, 200, 1000)
```

You made a triangle that moved around! Feel free to change the numbers to speed up or slow down the shape.

END OF CHAPTER CHALLENGE

Write a program that includes the following:

- GraphicsWindow.BrushColor,
- GraphicsWindow.DrawEllipse,
- GraphicsWindow.FillEllipse,
- GraphicsWindow.FillTriangle,
- GraphicsWindow.FillRectangle,
- Shapes.AddTriangle, and
- Shapes.Animate.

CHAPTER TWENTY: SUBROUTINES

To "call" means to demand or direct something. In normal English, this could be used like, "This calls for celebration!" In computers, a call is a direction by a main computer program to execute the tasks of a subprogram (a smaller program inside of and used by a larger program). More specifically, a "call" is when a program temporarily transfers control of the computer to a subprogram. Once the subprogram is done executing, control of the computer is returned to the main program. A program could make many "calls" to multiple subprograms as the program does its sequence of tasks.

For example, if you were using a video game program, the video game program could call the "high score" subprogram after every game ended to make the words "High Score" pop up on the screen.

A function is a repeatable block of code that executes certain actions and performs tasks. You execute a function by calling it. This is also called "invoking" the function.

"Invoke" literally means to request or ask for something. In coding, it is to cause something to be carried out (performed).

There are other words in technology for this concept: method, subroutine, subprogram, procedure, routine.

KEYWORDS

There are certain words you can't use as variables. These are called reserved words or keywords. Examples of keywords are:

"True" and "False" – which are used in Python to show the result of a comparison. For example, a comparison that checks "is 4 bigger than 2?" would result in True.

The reason you cannot use reserved words (keywords) is that they already mean something else – they are *reserved* for Small Basic.

CREATING A SUBROUTINE

Subroutines are started with the Sub keyword and ended with the EndSub keyword.

You execute a subroutine by calling the subroutine name followed by (). The parentheses tell the computer that the main program wants a subroutine executed.

To execute a subroutine, write and run this code:

```
TextWindow.Write("What is your name? ")
Name = TextWindow.Read()
TextWindow.Write("Hi there, " + Name + "! What time do you think it is? ")
Time = TextWindow.Read()
TextWindow.Write("Well " + Name + ", per your computer, the time now is actually: ")
PrintTime()
Sub PrintTime
  TextWindow.WriteLine(Clock.Time)
EndSub
```

You created a pretty cool subprogram!

In a larger program, subroutines become quite useful and save you from writing extra code because you can call the subroutine from anywhere in the program.

Subroutines can also be used to break apart large problems into smaller problems.

An important thing to keep in mind in writing code is the readability of your code – i.e., if another developer takes over after you, they need to know the purpose of different sections of your code. To clarify our code, we use "comments."

For example:

```
PrintTime()  'This is a subroutine that prints the current time
```

This is called "commenting your code."

In Small Basic, comments are preceded by an apostrophe ('). Comments are ignored by the computer and not executed.

To comment the code we wrote above, write this code:

```
TextWindow.Write("What is your name?: ")
'This allows the user to enter their name
Name = TextWindow.Read()
'This assigns what the user types to the variable Name
TextWindow.Write("Hi there, " + Name + "! What time do you think it is? ")
'This prints text and allows the user to guess the time
Time = TextWindow.Read()
'This assigns what the user types to the variable Time
TextWindow.Write("Well " + Name + ", per your computer, the time now is actually: ")
'This prints text
PrintTime()
'This names the subroutine
Sub PrintTime
'This starts the subroutine
TextWindow.WriteLine(Clock.Time)
'This accesses the computer's clock and returns the time
EndSub
'This ends the subroutine
```

END OF CHAPTER CHALLENGE

Complete the following:

Write your own program including a subroutine *and* comment your code.

CHAPTER TWENTY ONE: TURTLES

Write and execute this code:

```
Turtle.Show()
```

We bet the name of this chapter makes sense now!

You can move the turtle by entering in numbers inside parentheses (e.g., 1 means that the Turtle moves 1 pixel; Turtle.Move(50) means that the turtle moves 50 pixels).

Write and execute this code:

```
Turtle.Move(50)
Program.Delay(500)
Turtle.Move(25)
Program.Delay(500)
Turtle.Move(75)
Program.Delay(500)
Turtle.Move(35)
Program.Delay(500)
```

You made the turtle crawl up the screen!

TURTLE TRIANGLE

Now let's have the turtle draw a triangle by using the Angle property, which gets or sets the angle of the turtle.

Write and execute this code:

```
Turtle.Angle = 45
Turtle.Move(150)
Turtle.Angle = 135
Turtle.Move(150)
Turtle.Angle = 270
Turtle.Move(215)
```

Your little turtle drew a triangle!

TURNING TURTLE

We can also have the turtle turn right or left, change the colors and draw a rectangle!

Write and execute this code:

```
GraphicsWindow.BackgroundColor = "LightYellow"
GraphicsWindow.PenColor = "Magenta"
Turtle.Move(100)
Turtle.TurnRight()
Turtle.Move(200)
Turtle.TurnRight()
Turtle.Move(100)
Turtle.TurnRight()
Turtle.Move(200)
```

OCTAGON LOOP

Shapes can be drawn using a For Loop. Let's do an octagon.

Write and execute this code:

```
For X = 1 To 8
  Turtle.Move(75)
  Turtle.Turn(45)
EndFor
```

Do you see how this code works?

TURTLE CIRCLE

Let's make a shape that's virtually a circle. We will also use the X and Y Coordinates to place the turtle where we want it in the Graphics Window. And to make it more fun, let's randomize some colors! It's about to get trippy...

Write and execute this code:

```
Turtle.X = 20
Turtle.Y = 200
Sides = 200
Angle = 360 / Sides
Size = 1000 / Sides
For A = 1 To Sides
   GraphicsWindow.PenColor = GraphicsWindow.GetRandomColor()
   GraphicsWindow.BackgroundColor = GraphicsWindow.GetRandomColor()
   Turtle.Move(Size)
   Turtle.Turn(Angle)
EndFor
```

Since we used the GetRandomColor() operation, the sequence of colors (including the final background color) will change each time you run the program.

END OF CHAPTER CHALLENGE 1

Complete the following:

Using what you learned so far, have the turtle make a square using a For Loop. Additionally, have a background color, a pen color and try to make the square as centered as you can.

END OF CHAPTER CHALLENGE 2

Write a program that includes the following:

- Turtle.Show,
- Turtle.Move,
- Turtle.TurnRight,
- Turtle.Angle,
- Turtle.TurnLeft, and
- Turtle.MoveTo.

CHAPTER TWENTY TWO
MORE SUBROUTINES

We can also use subroutines to handle variables.

Write and execute this code:

```
TextWindow.Write("Type a number: ")
Number_1 = TextWindow.ReadNumber()
TextWindow.Write("Type another number: ")
Number_2 = TextWindow.ReadNumber()
TextWindow.Write("Now type another number: ")
Number_3 = TextWindow.ReadNumber()
TextWindow.Write("And one last number: ")
Number_4 = TextWindow.ReadNumber()
Largest_Number()
TextWindow.WriteLine("The largest number is: " + Largest_Number)
Sub Largest_Number
 If Number_1 > Number_2 And Number_1 > Number_3 And Number_1 > Number_4 Then
  Largest_Number = Number_1
 ElseIf Number_2 > Number_1 And Number_2 > Number_3 And Number_2 > Number_4 Then
  Largest_Number = Number_2
 ElseIf Number_3 > Number_1 And Number_3 > Number_2 And Number_3 > Number_4 Then
  Largest_Number = Number_3
 Else
  Largest_Number = Number_4
 EndIf
EndSub
```

You created a program that figures out the largest number typed by a user!

SOUNDS

Now let's try another subprogram that will be called three times and play sound! Make sure your computer volume is up high enough to hear.

We can play sound by using the Sound() object. The PlayClick(), PlayChime() and PlayBellRing() operations can be used with the Sound() object to play clicks, chimes and bell rings respectively!

Write and execute this subprogram:

```
TextWindow.BackgroundColor = "DarkRed"
TextWindow.WriteLine("This program allows you to choose from various sounds you'd like to hear.")
TextWindow.WriteLine("You'll get to choose three times!")
Sound()
  Sub Sound
  Start:
  TextWindow.WriteLine("To hear a bell ring, type Bell.")
  TextWindow.WriteLine("To hear a chime, type Chime.")
  TextWindow.WriteLine("To hear a click sound, type Click: ")
  Sound_Choice = TextWindow.Read()
    If Sound_Choice = "Bell" Then
      Sound.PlayBellRing()
    ElseIf Sound_Choice = "Chime" Then
      Sound.PlayChime()
    ElseIf Sound_Choice = "Click" Then
      Sound.PlayClick()
    Else
      TextWindow.WriteLine("Please type Chime, Bell or Click.")
      Goto Start
    EndIf
  EndSub
Sound()
Sound()
```

Now you may have had some issues with this subprogram. For example, if you typed "click" (all lowercase) instead of "Click" (capitalized), no sound played!

We can fix this by converting all user input (regardless of capitalization or lack of it) to lowercase, using the Text object with the ConvertToLowerCase() operation.

Write and execute this code:

```
TextWindow.BackgroundColor = "DarkBlue"
TextWindow.ForegroundColor = "White"
TextWindow.Write("This program allows you to choose from various sounds you'd wish to hear.")
TextWindow.WriteLine("You'll get to choose five times! ")
Sound()
Sub Sound
  Start:
  TextWindow.WriteLine("To hear a bell ring, type Bell.")
  TextWindow.WriteLine("To hear chimes, type Chimes.")
  TextWindow.WriteLine("To hear a click sound, type Click: ")
  Sound_Choice = TextWindow.Read()

  If (Text.ConvertToLowerCase(Sound_Choice) = "bell") Then
    Sound.PlayBellRing()
  ElseIf (Text.ConvertToLowerCase(Sound_Choice) = "chimes") Then
    Sound.PlayChimes()
  ElseIf (Text.ConvertToLowerCase(Sound_Choice) = "click") Then
    Sound.PlayClick()
  Else
    TextWindow.Write("Please type Chimes, Bell or Click.")
    Goto Start
  EndIf
EndSub
Sound()
Sound()
Sound()
Sound()
```

Now you don't have to worry how users type their answers! And you also made the program run five times through *and* changed the chime sound to chimes.

END OF CHAPTER CHALLENGE

Perform the following:

Create a subroutine that includes variables.

CHAPTER TWENTY THREE
ARRAYS

An array is a collection of data, arranged so that each piece of data in the collection can be individually identified. In computers, an array is a group of related things that are stored together in a sequence. It is a way things can be organized in a computer in a logical way. Arrays can be quite simple, or quite complex.

A simple array would be something like the numbers 7, 3 and 15. It would be written out like this:
[7, 3, 15]

These three pieces of data are called elements - they are the elements of the array.

A system is needed for identifying each element of an array. This is done by labeling each position in the array. The simplest method for this is to start numbering them at zero starting at the left position and counting up from there.

It is important to understand that the index only tells the position of the element in the array, and *not* the value of the element at that position.

In the above example, the element with a value of "7" would be at position 0, the element with a value of "3" would be at position 1, and the element with a value of "15" would be at position 2.

Another word for the position of an element is the "index" of the element - for the above example of an array, the element at index 0 has a value of "7," the element at index 1 has a value of "3," etc.

Each element, therefore, has two properties: its index and its value.

As another example, let's say you have three pictures of your cat, and you could save them in an array: CatPic1, CatPic 2, and CatPic 3. Here,the element at index 1 has a value of "CatPic2."

NAMES AND AGES

Write and execute this code:

```
TextWindow.Write("Enter the name of a person: ")
Name_1 = TextWindow.Read()
TextWindow.Write("Thanks! How old are they? ")
Age_1 = TextWindow.Read()
TextWindow.Write("Enter the name of a person: ")
Name_2 = TextWindow.Read()
TextWindow.Write("Thanks! How old are they? ")
Age_2 = TextWindow.Read()
TextWindow.Write("Enter the name of a person: ")
Name_3 = TextWindow.Read()
TextWindow.Write("Thanks! How old are they? ")
Age_3 = TextWindow.Read()
TextWindow.Write("Enter the name of a person: ")
Name_4 = TextWindow.Read()
TextWindow.Write("Thanks! How old are they? ")
Age_4 = TextWindow.Read()
TextWindow.WriteLine("Well done! Here is the list:")
TextWindow.WriteLine(Name_1 + " is " + Age_1 + " years young! ")
TextWindow.WriteLine(Name_2 + " is " + Age_2 + " years young! ")
TextWindow.WriteLine(Name_3 + " is " + Age_3 + " years young! ")
TextWindow.WriteLine(Name_4 + " is " + Age_4 + " years young! ")
```

Well done on creating this program!

CREATING AN ARRAY

The last program we wrote isn't an array, but we can write the code as an array. By using an array, we can replace the need for creating the variables (Name_1, Name_2, Name_3, Name_4, Age_1, Age_2, etc.).

Instead, we can use an index to store the names and ages. Each input is an index for the array and is stored as one variable. Storing values in an array allows you to access arrays inside of loops. The easiest way to show this is to write the code.

Write and execute this code:

```
For A = 1 To 4
  TextWindow.WriteLine("Please enter the name for person " + A + ": ")
  Name[A] = TextWindow.Read()
EndFor
For B = 1 To 4
  TextWindow.WriteLine("What is person " + B + "'s age?: ")
  Age[B] = TextWindow.Read()
EndFor
TextWindow.Write("Hello, ")
For A = 1 To 4
  TextWindow.Write(Name[A])
  If A < 3 Then
    TextWindow.Write(", ")
  ElseIf A < 4 Then
    TextWindow.Write(" and ")
  EndIf
EndFor
TextWindow.Write("! You are ")
For B = 1 To 4
  TextWindow.Write(Age[B])
  If B < 3 Then
    TextWindow.Write(", ")
  ElseIf B < 4 Then
    TextWindow.Write(" and ")
  Else
    TextWindow.Write(" respectively.")
  EndIf
EndFor
TextWindow.WriteLine("")
```

In the above code, "A" and "B" are referred to as the operators. Our indices are 1 to 4 and visually would look something like this:

Indic es	1	2	3	4

99

A (Name)	Name entered by user	Name entered by user	Name entered by user	Name entered by user
B (Age)	Age entered by user	Age entered by user	Age entered by user	Age entered by user

Let's write another array.

Write and execute this code:

```
TextWindow.Write("What is your name? ")
Input["Name"] = TextWindow.Read()
TextWindow.Write("How tall are you? ")
Input["Height"] = TextWindow.Read()
TextWindow.Write("What year were you born? ")
Input["Birth_year"] = TextWindow.Read()
TextWindow.Write("What is your favorite color? ")
Input["Color"] = TextWindow.Read()
TextWindow.Write("What country were you born in? ")
Input["Country"] = TextWindow.Read()
TextWindow.Write("Please type one of the following to pull relevant data: ")
TextWindow.WriteLine("Name, Height, Birth_year, Color or Country. ")
Index = TextWindow.Read()
TextWindow.WriteLine("The " + Index + " you entered is " + Input[Index] + "!")
```

DATA STRUCTURE

To fully understand arrays, you must know what a "data structure" is. A data structure refers to the organization of related pieces of information. There are different data structures that each allow different operations to be performed on the data. A data structure refers to how the data is organized in terms of implementation (use of the data; relation of the various parts of the data). It is a particular way to organize data in a computer so that it can be used efficiently.

Data structures are used as a means of organizing information in a computer so that the data can be utilized in an efficient manner.

For example, consider two different areas of business:
1) The shipping industry, and
2) The manufacturing industry.

The types of data the shipping industry may need to collect and organize will center around vehicles and their capacity, shipping rates, fuel costs, travel times between various geographical points, etc.

The types of data the manufacturing industry may need to collect and organize will center around raw materials, product manufacturing methods and times, inventory locations and amounts, shipping information, etc.

The structure of the data used by computers in these two industries may have similarities, but it's certain that the data structures won't be identical.

A linear data structure is simply a data structure where the data in the structure are organized one after the other – basically a list.

For example, a list of the states in the U.S. Each element of the structure, conceptually, comes right before or after another element.

When speaking about arrays, "dimension" has a specific meaning. A one-dimensional array is a linear data structure. The last program you wrote was a one-dimensional array.

A two-dimensional array is basically an array of arrays. Essentially, you could think of this as a grid of rows and columns, where each entry in the grid is itself an array. You will explore this further in the next chapter.

END OF CHAPTER CHALLENGE

Complete the following:

Create your own one-dimensional array.

CHAPTER TWENTY FOUR
TWO-DIMENSIONAL ARRAYS

We will now write a two-dimensional array.

Write and execute this code:

```
Animals["Princess"]["Color"] = "Black"
Animals["Princess"]["Species"] = "Dog"
Animals["Ivy"]["Color"] = "Gray with dark spots and stripes"
Animals["Ivy"]["Species"] = "Cat"
Animals["Goldie"]["Color"] = "Gold"
Animals["Goldie"]["Species"] = "Fish"
Animals["Tweet"]["Color"] = "Green with yellow"
Animals["Tweet"]["Species"] = "Bird"
TextWindow.Write("What is the name? ")
Name = TextWindow.Read()
TextWindow.WriteLine("Their color is: " + Animals[Name]["Color"])
TextWindow.WriteLine("Their species is: " + Animals[Name]["Species"])
```

When the program runs, it will ask you for the name of the pet. Enter one of the four names (Princess, Ivy, Goldie, or Tweet).

Visually, this is what we created in our array:

Name:	Princess	Ivy	Goldie	Tweet
Color:	Black	Gray with dark spots and stripes	Gold	Green with yellow
Species:	Dog	Cat	Goldfish	Parakeet

ARRAYS AND GRAPHICS

Arrays can also be used with Graphics.

Write and execute this code:

```
GraphicsWindow.BackgroundColor = "Black"
GraphicsWindow.Height = 600
GraphicsWindow.Width = 605
Rows = 10
Columns = 10
Sides = 50
For A = 1 To Columns
  For B = 1 To Rows
    GraphicsWindow.BrushColor = "Blue"
    Squares[A][B] = Shapes.AddRectangle(Sides, Sides)
    Shapes.Move(Squares[A][B], A * Sides, B * Sides)
  EndFor
EndFor
```

END OF CHAPTER CHALLENGE

Complete the following:

Create your own two-dimensional array.

CHAPTER TWENTY FIVE: SOME BASIC PROGRAMS

Now we will put together some of what you've learned so far to make some basic programs. Feel free to customize some of these programs if you choose!

PROGRAM 1

Write and execute this code:

```
GraphicsWindow.BackgroundColor = "LightCyan"
GraphicsWindow.PenColor = "DarkSlateBlue"
GraphicsWindow.Width = 400
GraphicsWindow.Height = 400
For A = 1 To 200 Step 6
  GraphicsWindow.DrawRectangle(200 - A, 200 - A, A * 2, A * 2)
  Program.Delay(100)
EndFor
For A = 1 To 200 Step 6
  GraphicsWindow.DrawEllipse(200 - A, 200 - A, A * 2, A *2)
  Program.Delay(100)
EndFor
```

PROGRAM 2

Write and execute this code:

```
GraphicsWindow.Width = 1000
GraphicsWindow.Height = 650
GraphicsWindow.BackgroundColor = "Black"
A = 1000
B = 1000
For C = 1 To 100000
  D = Math.GetRandomNumber(3)
  E = 500
  Program.Delay(.1)
  F = 30
  If (D = 1) then
    E = 30
    F = 1000
    Program.Delay(.1)
  EndIf
  If (D = 2) Then
    E = 1000
    F = 1000
    Program.Delay(.1)
  EndIf
  A = (A + E) / 2
  Program.Delay(.1)
  B = (B + F) / 2
  Random_Color = GraphicsWindow.GetRandomColor()
  GraphicsWindow.SetPixel(A, B, Random_Color)
EndFor
```

PROGRAM 3

Write and execute this code:

```
GraphicsWindow.Title = "America!"
GraphicsWindow.Width = 1000
GraphicsWindow.Height = 600
For A = 1 To 100000
  GraphicsWindow.BrushColor = "Red"
  B = Math.GetRandomNumber(1000)
  C = Math.GetRandomNumber(1000)
  GraphicsWindow.FillEllipse(B, C, 4, 4)
EndFor
For D = 1 To 100000
  GraphicsWindow.BrushColor = "Blue"
  B = Math.GetRandomNumber(500)
  C = Math.GetRandomNumber(275)
  GraphicsWindow.FillEllipse(B, C, 4, 4)
EndFor
```

PROGRAM 4

Write and execute this code:

```
GraphicsWindow.Width = 275
Turtle.X = 130
Turtle.Y = 400
GraphicsWindow.PenColor = "Green"
Turtle.Move(150)
Turtle.X = 135
Turtle.Y = 400
GraphicsWindow.PenColor = "Green"
Turtle.Move(150)
Turtle.X = 100
Turtle.Y = 200
GraphicsWindow.PenColor = "MediumVioletRed"
Turns = 200
Length = 300 /  Turns
Angle = 400 / Turns
Turtle.Speed = 10
For A = 1 To 6
  For B = 1 To Turns
    Turtle.Move(Length)
    Turtle.Turn(Angle)
  EndFor
  Turtle.Turn(18)
EndFor
Turtle.X = 128.5
Turtle.Y = 193
```

PROGRAM 5

Write and execute this code:

```
GraphicsWindow.BackgroundColor = "DarkBlue"
GraphicsWindow.Height = 600
GraphicsWindow.Width = 605
Rows = 10
Columns = 10
Sides = 50
For A = 1 To Columns
  For B = 1 To Rows
    GraphicsWindow.BrushColor = GraphicsWindow.GetRandomColor()
    Squares[A][B] = Shapes.AddRectangle(Sides, Sides)
    Shapes.Move(Squares[A][B], A * Sides, B * Sides)
  EndFor
EndFor
For A = 1 To Columns
  For B = 1 To Rows
    Shapes.Animate(Squares[B][A], 300, 0, 1000)
    Program.Delay(50)
  EndFor
EndFor

For A = 1 To Columns
  For B = 1 To Rows
    Shapes.Animate(Squares[B][A], 288, 500, 1000)
    Program.Delay(10)
  EndFor
EndFor
For A = 1 To Columns
  For B = 1 To Rows
    Shapes.Animate(Squares[B][A], 275, 250, 1000)
    Program.Delay(10)
  EndFor
EndFor
```

CHAPTER TWENTY SIX: EVENTS

An event is an action or something that occurs that is detected by a computer program. There can be system events (events that occur as a result of operations the computer does automatically) or user events (like typing on the keyboard or clicking a mouse).

In Small Basic, an event is something that reacts to a user's action and is when the computer tells you that something interesting has happened. For example, if you make a program that turns the screen blue when you click on the word "blue," clicking on the word "blue" would be the event.

Events can make programs more interesting and interactive.

Interactive means that two things influence one another and create effects on each other. In computers, interactive refers to a computer that is able to be communicated with and gotten to perform activities by a human; these activities involve the person using the computer. An interactive computer is a computer that you can affect in some way (move a pointer on a screen and select something, etc.) and which will respond in some manner. Most, if not all, computers you've used have been interactive.

The computer game "Hangman" could be developed in Small Basic and would include events. In this game, the user makes choices, and the program receives the user's input using events. You can find code for Hangman games written in Small Basic online, simply by Googling "Hangman Small Basic" or some such search term.

There is such a thing as "event-driven programming." This is programming where the flow of the program is controlled by events. An example would be a program in which the program flow (how the program progresses) is determined by the typing of keys and clicking the mouse.

Write and execute this code:

```
GraphicsWindow.DrawBoundText(250, 200, 100, "Click the screen!")
GraphicsWindow.MouseDown = Click
GraphicsWindow.BrushColor = "Yellow"
GraphicsWindow.BackgroundColor = "Black"
Sub Click
  GraphicsWindow.ShowMessage("You clicked the mouse!", "NOTICE")
  A = GraphicsWindow.MouseX - 5
  B = GraphicsWindow.MouseY - 5
  GraphicsWindow.FillTriangle(A, B, 30, 30, 40, 40)
EndSub
```

There are two chunks of text following ShowMessage. The first chunk is what will be displayed inside the window, and the second chunk is what is displayed at the top.

This program contains a subroutine as well. Every time the user clicks in the GraphicsWindow, the subroutine "Click" is called. The Click subroutine results in a couple events:

111

1. A message pops up, and
2. A yellow ray expands out from the top left corner after you shut the message box.

One of the unique things about events is that when an event occurs, the subroutine is called automatically.

In the above code, we assigned the subroutine name to the MouseDown event which is connected to the GraphicsWindow object. Even though the MouseDown looks like a property (attributes of an object), we are actually assigning the subroutine "Click" to it. If MouseDown were a property, we would be assigning it a value (as opposed to a subroutine).

PAINT

Now that you are familiar with subroutines, events, and other key coding concepts, we can create our very own "Paint" program that will allow you to draw using the mouse. You will be able to draw in rainbow-like colors with a thick brush.

In this next program, we will be using the MouseMove event, which gets the X and Y coordinates, in pixels, of the mouse cursor – based on where it is as compared to the top left of the desktop.

Write and execute this code:

```
GraphicsWindow.MouseMove = A
GraphicsWindow.MouseDown = B
GraphicsWindow.BackgroundColor = "SkyBlue"
GraphicsWindow.PenWidth = (25)
Sub B
  C = GraphicsWindow.MouseX
  D = GraphicsWindow.MouseY
EndSub
Sub A
  E = GraphicsWindow.MouseX
  F = GraphicsWindow.MouseY
  If (Mouse.IsLeftButtonDown) Then
    GraphicsWindow.PenColor = GraphicsWindow.GetRandomColor()
    GraphicsWindow.DrawLine(C, D, E, F)
  EndIf
C = E
D = F
EndSub
```
'Click and hold down mouse as you move it around.

<u>END OF CHAPTER CHALLENGE</u>

Create a program that includes the following events:

- MouseUp,
- MouseDown,
- MouseMove,
- KeyDown, and
- KeyUp.

CHAPTER TWENTY SEVEN: THE FINAL SECTION

Now that you know the fundamentals of Small Basic, you will now do some coding exercises that may require you to do some online research.

SMALL BASIC EXERCISE 1

Complete the following:

Create a program that returns the smaller of two numbers entered by a user. The program should receive two different numbers chosen by the user and then display the smaller of the two.

For example: The user inputs 21 and 3, and the program returns the number 3.

Hint:
• If statements

SMALL BASIC EXERCISE 2

The company you work for just opened two new branches. One is in New York City, the other in London. They need a very simple program to find out if the branches are open or closed based on the current time of the Headquarters here in Portland. The hours of both branches are 9:00 a.m.–9:00 p.m. in their own time zone.

Complete the following:

Create a program that will determine whether the London and New York offices are open or closed based on the current time of the HQ in Portland. Have the program display if each of the two branches is open or closed.

Hints:
- Clock.Time class (Clock.Hour operates on a 24-hour clock)
- If statements

SMALL BASIC EXERCISE 3

Your employer wants a program to copy a .txt file from one folder to another.

Complete the following:

Create two folders on your desktop. Create one text file inside one of the folders (leaving the other folder empty).

Your task is to use Small Basic to copy the file from the folder it is stored in and place the copy in the empty folder.

Note: In Windows, to obtain the file path, hold shift and right click on the file and then choose "copy as path."

Hint:
- File.CopyFile Method

SMALL BASIC EXERCISE 4

Your employer now wants a program that will copy a .txt file from one folder to another only if the London office is closed.

Complete the following:

Using the same two folders created in Exercise 3, make a program that copies a file from the folder it is stored in and place it in the other folder ONLY if the London office is closed.

Hint:
- It's okay to reuse code you wrote in Exercises 2 and 3.

SMALL BASIC EXERCISE 5

Your employer loves the program you just created but now wants it to have a simple graphical user interface (GUI) for other employees to use. Note: a GUI is a representation of the various objects in a computer – files, programs, etc. – in a graphical form. That is, it presents the user with pictures and diagrams that communicate the things on the computer and their arrangement.

Complete the following:

Make a simple GUI for your program. All it needs to have is a button in the middle that, when clicked, copies a file from one folder to another ONLY if the London office is closed.

Hint:
- Make the code you wrote in Exercise 4 a subroutine that is called when a button is clicked.

www.ingramcontent.com/pod-product-compliance
Lightning Source LLC
LaVergne TN
LVHW081530050326

832903LV00025B/1709